Outreach Training Workbook

URBAN ASSAULT SERIES

The WORD ON THE STREET

Outreach Training Workbook

JDMorgan

ELEVENTH HOUR
PUBLISHING HOUSE

Urban Assault; The Word On The Street
Outreach Training Workbook

Editors: Richard Blake, Brenda Walker
Artwork, design and layout: Creative by Design

All Scripture references are from the King James Version unless otherwise specified

Copyright © 2016 James D. Morgan
All Rights Reserved
Eleventh Hour Publishing House
Visalia, CA 93277
ISBN : 978-0-9898577-1-0
Printed in the United States of America

CONTENTS

Introduction
About Urban Assault Outreach Training
How to Use this Manual

Section One: The Word on the Street
The Kingdom Agenda 1
Jesus in the 'Hood 2
Into the Street 3
The Needful NOW 4

Section Two: Empowered Equipped Engaged
Power with a Purpose 13
Christian Catalysis 16
The Fear Factor 17

Section Three: The Mission The Method The Message
By Any Means 25
Relational Evangelism 26
The Harvest Principle 27

Section Four: Hood-ology
Contextual Evangelism 35
Sharing the Faith 39
Common Objections/Biblical Responses 44
Tactical Tips 46

ESP^P 57

Section Five: The Ministry of Prayer
The Ministry of Prayer 63

Section Six: Defending the Faith
The Urban Apologetic 71

Introduction
The Urban Apologetic

The term apologetics is derived from the Greek word *apologia*, which means to defend or to vindicate. In ancient courts of law, when a plaintiff brought an accusation against someone, that person was allotted time for a rebuttal or defense in response to the charge. In its early years, Christianity came under intense scrutiny and attack from philosophers and religious sects as Jesus was introduced as the Son of God and the Savior of an increasingly pagan world. As a result, it became necessary for those who were well versed in the Faith to establish a relevant response based in historic fact and sound reasoning. Among the early apologists were Justin Martyr, Irenaeus of Lyons, Augustine of Hippo, and Clement of Alexandria. I would add to that list those I consider to be the great apologists of our era; C.S. Lewis, Josh McDowell and Dr. Ravi Zacharias.

When I consider the unique way of life in the inner-city ghetto, I am convinced that a new standard of defending the faith is called for—the Urban Apologetic. If there is no such term as urban apologetics, perhaps there should be, because there is a marked difference between the urban and suburban cultures.

America's urban centers are in crisis! Our inner cities lead the nation in felony and drug arrests, violent crime and AIDS related illnesses. Every 69 seconds, a baby is born to an unmarried mother; every 11 minutes a juvenile is arrested for a violent crime; every 4 hours a child is killed by a gun, and youth violence takes more than twice as many American lives every year as cancer, heart disease, and car accidents combined.[1]

Racism, poverty, corrupt leaders, dysfunctional or non-existent families, under-funded schools and over-funded prisons have created an environment where people have become hardened to a lifestyle of drug dealing and prostitution as the most viable means of income. Here, the incarceration of so many marginalized citizens has given birth to a culture where kindness is equated with weakness and where violence has become a means of gaining power and respect.

And at the heart of this crisis, God has positioned his church as a witness.

In urban centers across America, Christian churches occupy almost every corner; many in neighborhoods where violent crime, abject poverty and substance abuse have become accepted facts of life. Yet, many pastors believe that a major short coming of the urban church is the lack of evangelism.[2]

In order to capture (or re-capture) the relevance of the gospel message to the inner city, we must accept the challenge to move out of the confines of our sanctuaries—not just in preaching, singing and handing out tracts—but in touching the lives of those that God has charged us to "bring in hither".

We have developed this study because America's urban centers present a different and more challenging demographic than the more socially acceptable "norm" of the suburbs.

We pray that as you complete this study, you will be motivated to move out of the comfort zone of the sanctuary into "the streets and lanes of the city". There is an urgent need to reach the inner city, and God has a plan to engage an empowered church and impassioned believers... like you.

Urban Assault Outreach Training Modules

These training modules are the result of outreach/evangelism strategies and trainings gathered from across the country in seminars and through more than twenty years of field experience in the ministry of urban evangelism.

While the principles taught in this study are Bible-based and universal in scope, we must also acknowledge those who laid the foundation upon which this work has been built: Dr. Billy Graham, Prof. Flavil Yeakley, Dr. Ravi Zaccharias, Paul E. Little, Mark Guy Pearse, Josh McDowell, Bill Bright and Lee Stroebel along with practical biblical applications from Bishop J. W. Macklin, Bishop Bob Jackson, Pastor A. J. Latchison, Pastor A. Wayne Jones, Evangelist Ron Haynes and Evangelist Drusilla Williams.

Urban Assault Outreach Training focuses exclusively on sharing the faith in the urban context, and has been adapted for use by local churches, individuals and mission groups. While this book is not exhaustive, its training modules offer a concise and coherent package of witnessing tools. These activity-based lessons empower the Believer to effectively share the faith individually and corporately witnessing, to develop skills for identifying and approaching potential seekers, to answer common objections and challenges to the Faith, and to ultimately lead a seeker to salvation through prayer.

In this course, students will practice ways to open conversations in a natural fashion and make a clear presentation of the Gospel message with an emphasis on empathy. They will learn how to avoid negative confrontations and arguments, and how to draw conclusions and decisions more effectively. Students will learn a simple "Cognitive Discernment" technique to assess their surroundings, gauge the receptiveness of the listener, and learn when to persist or when to plant a seed and make a tactical withdrawal.

Equipped with the Bible-based information in this study, the serious student will gain Scriptural knowledge, communication skills and learn practical approaches that will empower them to impact individuals and communities with the Gospel of Jesus Christ.

HOW TO USE THIS MANUAL

To get the best possible results from these studies and exercises, we recommend that you approach each lesson prayerfully, examining the corresponding Scriptures.

Take advantage of the ample space in the margins and the blank pages to record your thoughts and reflections on the subject matter.

Be sure to fill in the blank spaces in the Review section to internalize and remember key concepts and Bible verses.

If you are teaching as a course or studying in a group, you may want to engage in role playing as prospect and evangelist; sharing the message of salvation and leading in the Salvation prayer, using the examples from the exercises.

We've included the ESP^p Evangelistic Styles Personailty Profile as a method to discover your best potential approach in sharing The Faith.

Please note: this exercise is not scientific, but only a best assessment of your personality based on your accurate answers.

It is not intended in any way to restrict you to the evangelism style your answers may indicate.

In Defending The Faith, we've provided answers to many of the pressing challenges to what we believe. We do not advocate arguments and confrontations in sharing our faith, however, we do believe that Christians need to be "ready to give an answer" when our faith is challenged (1 Peter 3:15) which includes an apologetic defense of The Faith.

Our responses are not meant to provoke debate or argument, but to equip the Believer with "a reason of the hope that is in you"

Again, we pray that this study encourages and equips you for sharing The Faith in the urban context...in the streets and lanes of the city...and to the uttermost parts of the earth.

SECTION

The WORD On The Street

GOD'S CALL TO REACH THE CITIES

In this opening segment, we examine:
- God's Kingdom Agenda
- His command to reach out to the blind, the broken, and the bound
- God's urgent call to take the gospel to the streets of the city

As you begin, open your Bible and be prepared to read the corresponding Scriptures. Take advantage of the ample margin space and note section to write out your thoughts and reflections on the subject matter. Be sure to fill in the blank spaces with the appropriate answers.

THE KINGDOM AGENDA

Background Scriptures:
Eph. 1:4-5; 1 Tim. 1:9; 2 Cor. 5:18

From Genesis to Revelation, the Bible carries one theme and one thought;

GOD RECONCILING THE WORLD TO HIMSELF THROUGH JESUS CHRIST.

The Old Testament details man's fall from Grace and God's promise of a Messiah. The New Testament records the coming of the Messiah, and the completion of God's plan of salvation through Jesus Christ.

GOD'S AGENDA

God's command to his disciples (the church) is to move from the comfort of the sanctuary and take the message of salvation to every living soul.

When we fully grasp the reality that before time began, God had no other agenda than to reconcile mankind to Himself—and to engage us as ministers of reconciliation—it will transform the nature of our relationship with Him; give true meaning and depth to our worship experience; provide definition for our church auxiliaries and motivate us to move beyond the four walls of our churches and into the *Highways and Hedges.*

"According as he hath chosen us in him before the foundation of the world..."
Eph. 1:4-5

"Who hath saved us, and called us with an holy calling, not according to our works, but according to his own purpose and grace, which was given us in Christ Jesus before the world began."
2 Timothy 1:9

"Now all things are of God who has reconciled us to Himself through Jesus Christ, and has given unto us the ministry of reconciliation."
2 Corinthians 5:18

Jesus in the 'Hood

(How does God see your neighborhood?)

Background Scripture–John 4: 4-10; 25-29

"And he must needs go through Samaria."

John 4:4

Samaria was the ghetto of that era, the 'hood.

This was the place that religious people avoided. The organized church had given up on Samaria and the upright used an alternate route to bypass the area altogether. Yet, Jesus saw this as the ideal place to share the Good News of Salvation.

He didn't focus on the sin of the city.

He didn't complain about the depravity or corruption.

Jesus looked beyond all the things we would call unclean and ungodly, and saw people in need of ...

SALVATION.

"..behold, I say unto you, lift up your eyes and look on the fields for they are white already to harvest." John 4:35

In sharing his vision with his disciples, Jesus challenged them to share his point of view; "lift up your eyes and look".

No matter how economically depressed, drug infested or crime-ridden, Jesus sees your neighborhood as a field "white" or ripe for the harvesting.

In the midst of the poverty, corruption, crime and apparent hopelessness, someone is waiting to hear the liberating Gospel of Jesus Christ.

God has strategically placed us to impact the lives around us, and we have the responsibility to show them the way to life;

JESUS

INTO THE STREET

"...Go out quickly into the streets and lanes of the city, and bring in hither the poor, and the maimed, and the halt, and the blind." Luke 14:21b

In this passage of Scripture, Jesus commands the disciples (his church) to take the gospel out of the sanctuary and into the streets.

His focus—

The Poor:

The unemployed or unemployable; people who had little hope, people who depended on others for their daily needs, people whose will to succeed had been broken, people whose dignity and self respect had been stripped away.

The Maimed:

Those persons who have not only been wounded, but who have been beaten to the point of mutilation, disfigured by life's hardships.

The Halt:

The crippled, stunted, hampered; these are the people whose potential has been hindered by circumstance beyond their control.

The Blind:

Those who are unable (and sometimes unwilling) to see.

"The Spirit of the Lord is upon me, because He hath anointed me to preach the gospel to the poor; He hath sent me to heal the brokenhearted, to preach deliverance to the captives, and recovery of sight to the blind, to set at liberty them that are bruised." Luke 4:18

The Word of God challenges us to focus our efforts and attentions on those around us who have not discovered the Abundant Life; to roll up our spiritual sleeves, move out of the comfort of the Sanctuary, and literally reach out and touch the lives of the outcast and the downtrodden.

"For too much of American Christianity, to follow Jesus is to seek comfort devoid of courageous compassion and bold witness for 'the least of these.'"

West, Dr. Cornell. 1999. *Prophetic Christian Thought,.* Basic Civitas Books

THE NEEDFUL NOW

"...Go out quickly into the streets and lanes of the city."
Luke 14:21b

Again, in this passage of Scripture, Jesus commands the disciples to take the gospel out of the sanctuary and into the streets.

In this discussion, we want to point your attention to Jesus' use of the word "quickly".

In every account of the commissioning Scriptures, Jesus commands the disciples to go out. Yet in the gospel of Luke, Jesus expresses an urgency.

> Go out quickly.

The definition of the word *quickly* infers that time was of the essence, and Jesus was absolute in affirming that the need to take the message of salvation to the street was crucial and immediate. And today, as crime and poverty rates increase by the hour and the destabilization of the urban family has become an accepted fact of life, and as the drug culture has entrenched itself in our urban centers, that same sense of urgency calls out to us from inner cities across America. And the need to take the message of salvation to the streets of the city is crucial and immediate.

" The Lord is not slack concerning his promise, as some men count slackness; but is longsuffering to usward, not willing that any should perish, but that all should come to repentance."
2 Peter 3:9

"Go ye therefore and teach all nations." Matthew 28:19

"Go ye into all the world and preach the Gospel to every creature." Mark 16:15

"Go out into the highways and hedges and compel them to come in..." Luke 14:23

"...one third of all African American men aged eighteen to thirty-four are under the supervision of the criminal justice system- either in jail or prison, on probation or parole, or awaiting trial."

Mauer, Marc. September 1994. *Americans Behind Bars: The International Use of Incarceration*, 1992-93. Washington, D.C.: The Sentencing Project.

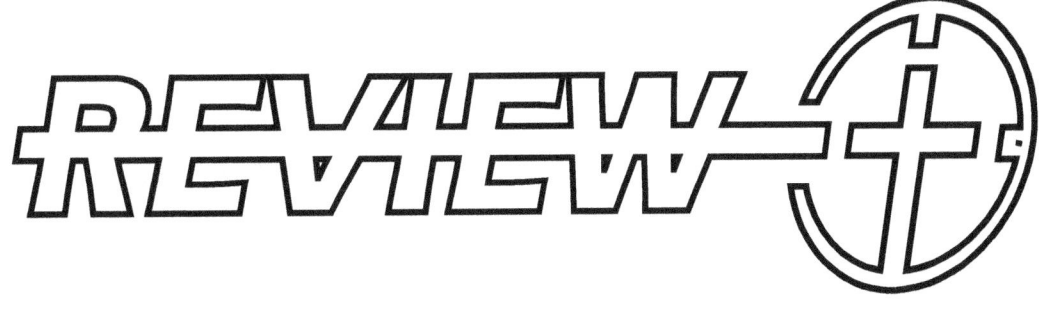

The Kingdom Agenda

1. The Bible carries one theme and one thought_____
   _____.

2. The Old Testament details man's fall from Grace and God's promise of a_____. The New Testament records the coming of the Messiah, and the completion of _____.

3. God's command to his disciples (the church) is to move from the comfort of _____ and take the message of_____ to every living soul.

4. God has had no other agenda than_____ and to engage us as _____.

JESUS IN THE 'HOOD

1. In sharing his vision with his disciples, Jesus challenged them to share _____
   _____.

2. Jesus saw Samaria as the ideal place to share _____
   _____.

3. Jesus looked beyond all the things we would call unclean and ungodly, and saw _____ in need of _____.

4. God has strategically placed you where you are to _____
   _____.

INTO THE STREET

1. Jesus commands the disciples (his _____) to move out into the _____ and lanes of the city.

2. What was Jesus' focus?
   The _____, the _____, the _____, and the _____.

3. The Word of God challenges us to focus our _____ and _____ on those around us who have not discovered the Abundant Life.

4. The Word challenges us to move out of the _____ of the _____, and literally reach out and touch the lives of the _____ and the _____.

THE NEEDFUL NOW

1. In the gospel of Luke, Jesus expresses an urgency _____.

2. The definition of the word *quickly* suggests that time was of the essence, and Jesus was absolute in affirming the need to take the message of_____ to the street was crucial and _____.

3. Today the need to take the message of salvation to the streets of the city is _____.

4. "_____ ye therefore and teach all nations." Matthew _____

5. "_____ ye into all the world and preach the Gospel to every creature." Mark _____

6. "_____ out into the highways and hedges and compel them to come in." Luke _____

SECTION 2

EMPOWERED
EQUIPPED
ENGAGED

POWER TO IMPACT YOUR WORLD

God has provided everything we need to become effective soul winners.
In this segment, you will discover:
- The purpose for God's indwelling Spirit in the believer
- The impact of your influence as a Christian
- How to overcome fear of sharing The Faith

POWER WITH A PURPOSE

"Ye shall receive power, after that the Holy Ghost is come upon you, and ye shall be witnesses unto me both in Jerusalem, and in all Judea, and in Samaria, and unto the uttermost part of the earth." Acts 1:8

The most effective witness to any event is an eyewitness. The testimony of an eyewitness is the only admissible evidence in a U.S. court of law. All second hand information is dismissed as hearsay.

The same rule applies in Christian evangelism and witnessing. Your testimony of the saving reality of Jesus Christ is only as effective as your eyewitness experience.

God's indwelling Spirit moves you from an intellectual (think-so) acquaintance with the historical facts to an experiential (know-so) relationship with a risen Savior.

Religion, philosophy, and morality can be argued from any given point of view. The one issue that cannot be argued or refuted is the personal testimony of God's Power, manifested in your life.

Recognize the Power of your Testimony

>YOU ARE ONLY AS CONVINCING AS YOU ARE...
>
>CONVINCED
>
>YOU ARE ONLY AS PERSUASIVE AS YOU ARE...
>
>PERSUADED

"For we have not followed cunningly devised fables, when we made known unto you the coming of our Lord Jesus Christ , but were eyewitnesses of his majesty."
   2 Peter 1:16

The most powerful weapon in your witnessing arsenal is your personal testimony; your eyewitness account of God's power to save.

Your first hand experience of the reality of Jesus Christ empowers you to become an effective witness. God's indwelling Spirit (Acts 1:8) moves you from an intellectual agreement with the biblical facts to a *know-so* relationship with a risen Savior.

THE POWER IN YOUR TESTIMONY

Testifying, in the context of evangelism, is not about relaying a personal experience of visions, miraculous events, or revelations. When you share your testimony for the purpose of reaching a soul, your prime objective is to tell a credible story of your conversion experience:

1. What my life was like before I met Jesus.

2. How I came to know Jesus.

3. How my life has changed since I've met Jesus.

PRACTICE SHARING YOUR TESTIMONY

1. What my life was like before I met Jesus. (*Feelings, attitude, habits, actions or relationships*)

2. What happened to make me start thinking about God/Jesus as the answer to my problems. (*Someone who shared the Faith, a singular event that impacted your life*)

3. What finally moved me to accept Jesus as Savior. (*The reality of the Word, a moment of clarity, the reality of God*)

4. What actually changed in my life, after receiving Jesus. (*Changed behavior, attitudes, appetites, etc.*)

5. What have the benefits been, since I received Jesus as Savior. (*Peace of mind, freedom from addictions or guilt, new outlook on life*)

Christian Catalysis

Catalyst- A chemical or substance that causes or accelerates a chemical reaction without itself being affected. A person or thing that precipitates change. Catalysis- The acceleration or slowing of a chemical reaction by the action of a material which is recovered unchanged by the end of the reaction.

You are God's preserving virtue, and possibly the only contact some people will ever have with the gospel.

We are insulated, but not isolated.

In the Gospel of St. John, Jesus prays for the Believer, not that we should be removed from the ungodly influences around us; but that we remain in the world and become a Godly influence, impacting everything around us.

We are effective without becoming infected.

God has deliberately left the Believer as light in this present darkness and He has empowered us to change the world through the Gospel of Jesus Christ.

" Ye are the salt of the earth..." Matthew 5:13

"I have set thee to be a light of the Gentiles, that thou shouldest be for salvation unto the ends of the earth." Acts 13:47

"I pray not that thou shouldest take them out of the world, but that Thou shouldest keep them from the evil." John 17:15

"That ye may be blameless and harmless, the sons of God, without rebuke, in the midst of a crooked and perverse nation, among whom ye shine as lights in the world." Phil. 2:15

THE FEAR FACTOR

Background Scripture Acts 4:13-31
"And now, Lord, behold their threatening: and grant unto thy servants, that with all boldness they may speak thy word." Acts 4:29

In the face of overt adversity, the disciples were emboldened by God's Spirit to speak truth to power in asserting the veracity of the gospel. They were faced with threats, angry mobs, conflict with the established church (the Synagogue) and with legal repercussions from angry magistrates.

Today, we do not face the challenge of legal actions, mob violence or resistance from religious organizations as we proclaim the gospel ...at least not quite yet! But we are nevertheless faced with fear, our personal fears; fear of rejection; fear of failure; fear of embarrassment.

Note that the disciples' prayer was not for deliverance from confrontation, but for boldness—some call it "Holy Boldness"— to further proclaim the gospel.

GOD ANSWERED THEIR PRAYER.

OVERCOMING THE FEAR FACTOR

REJECTION:
They're not responding to you as an individual, but to the Spirit of God in you. Take your ego out of the equation...it's not about you.

FAILURE:
Not getting a decision immediately is not a failure to reach that individual.

EMBARRASSMENT:
Live out your testimony. Don't testify beyond your experience/commitment. Remember, you are a new creature in Christ Jesus.

" And when they had prayed, the place was shaken where they were assembled together; and they were all filled with the Holy Ghost, and they spake the word of God with boldness." Acts 4:31

POWER WITH A PURPOSE

1. Your testimony of the saving reality of Jesus Christ is only as effective as your _____.

2. God's indwelling _____ moves you from an intellectual (_____) acquaintance with the historical facts to an experiential (_____) relationship with a risen Savior.

3. The one issue that cannot be argued or refuted is the _____ of God's power, manifested in your life.

4. You are only as convincing as you are _____.

5. You are only as persuasive as you are _____.

CHRISTIAN CATALYSIS

1. You are God's _____, and possibly the only contact some people will ever have with the _____.

2. We are _____, but not _____.

3. In the Gospel of St. John, Jesus prays for the _____, not that we should be removed from the ungodly influences around us; but that we remain in the world and become a _____.

4. We are _____ without becoming _____.

5. God has deliberately left the believer as _____ in this present darkness, and He has _____ us to change the world through the Gospel of Jesus Christ.

THE FEAR FACTOR

1. In the face of overt adversity, the disciples were emboldened by God's Spirit to speak _____.

2. The disciples' prayer was not for deliverance from confrontation, but for _____.

3. They're not responding to you as an individual, but to the _____.

4. Take your _____ out of the equation.

5. Not getting a _____ is not a failure to reach that individual.

6. Live out your _____.

7. Don't testify beyond your _____.

SECTION 6

The MISSION
The METHOD
The MESSAGE

RELATING A RELEVANT FAITH

The focus of this lesson is on sharing the Faith through building relationships.

In this study you will learn how to:
- Use your past experiences as a vehicle for witnessing
- Recognize your role in the soul-winning process
- Share the gospel through making caring connections

BY ANY MEANS

The Apostle Paul put his entire life's experience at God's disposal for the sole purpose of reaching the lost.

Paul was born a Hebrew, ordained a Pharisee, worked as a tent maker, known as a teacher, a writer, a counselor and a convict.

His broad range of experience made him uniquely able to relate to people in various walks of life.

Paul spoke the language of the religious community in order to direct the religious person to a saving knowledge of Jesus. He was able to relate the Gospel of liberation to those who were in bondage. He could converse in the language of the scholar to communicate the message of salvation to those who trusted in their intellect.

Paul understood the importance of developing a rapport with the hearer by being able to relate through common experience.

YOUR ABILITY TO EMPATHIZE OR RELATE TO AN UNBELIEVER WILL MAKE YOU UNIQUELY ABLE TO REACH THE HEART OF THAT PERSON WITH THE GOSPEL.

"Unto the Jews, I became as a Jew, that I might gain the Jews; to them that are under the law, as under the law, that I might gain them that are under the law; to them that are without the law, as without law (being not without law to God, but under the law to Christ) that I might gain them that are without the law. To the weak, became I as weak, that I might gain the weak: I am made all things to all men, that I might by all means save some."

1 Corinthians 9:19-22

PEOPLE DON'T CARE HOW MUCH YOU KNOW UNTIL THEY KNOW HOW MUCH YOU CARE

What part of your life's experience are you willing to put at God's disposal?

Relational Evangelism

Genuine evangelism springs from genuine concern about an individual.

Practiced approaches and insincere presentations are easily read in inner city streets.

Simply put; People can sense if you're not sincere.

The effort to reach a soul is actually an effort to respond to their individual needs with the Gospel.

Relational evangelism begins with the intent of developing a responsive relationship with the hearer; establishing a common bond of shared concern and caring on the part of the evangelist.

This type of evangelism transcends a prepared speech or practiced presentation and moves into the type of love for the lost that Jesus exemplifies in the Scriptures.

This type of evangelism also necessitates the development of a follow-up ministry, bringing the seeker into the fellowship of the Body, where they become part of the fellowship of believers and grow from

DECISION TO DISCIPLESHIP.

Evangelist Ron Haynes shares the story of a woman who went to share the Faith with a group of *Hippies*.

When she met the group, dressed in her customary Sunday attire, they turned a deaf ear to her message, and consequently didn't receive the good news of the gospel.

She went home, put on a blue jean skirt, a tie-dyed Dashiki and teased her hair into an "Afro". When she returned, the group was open to the gospel because she approached them at the level of their understanding and from a position that respected their culture. This sensitivity opened the door by saying, "I care about you; where you are, and as you are."

Without changing our *message*, we must adapt our *method* to meet people where they are at the point of their need.

THE HARVEST PRINCIPLE

God has given a season for the initial planting or sharing the Gospel. There is a time for watering, or cultivating that Word which has already been planted. And there is a time for harvesting; leading the seeker to a saving knowledge of Jesus Christ.

Everyone plays a part in God's Cycle of Harvest. Let God's Spirit lead you in understanding what your role is.

THE PLANTER/THE INITIAL ENCOUNTER

Yours is the privilege of making First Contact. You are the witness who boldly goes where no one has gone before.

THE WATERER/SHARING THE FAITH

Yours is the call to faithfully live out the witness before the world. The words of your testimony and your acts of kindness will cause the seeker to want to know Jesus.

THE HARVESTER/GOD GIVING THE INCREASE

Yours is the honor of leading the seeker in the Sinner's Prayer and ensuring they are connected to the Body of Christ.

" I have planted, Apollos watered; but God gave the increase".
1 Corinthians 3:6-7

Background Scripture study;
Matthew 13:19-23.

Often, the Christian witness is discouraged by the type of response, or failure to respond in the prospective seeker. Understand the response is based on their receptiveness, or the condition of their *soil*.

Some are not open to receive the gospel, some are stony hearted, others shallow, and still others become entangled with worldly living.

Remember, they are not responding to <u>you</u>. It is the Lord that draws the seeker, and prepares him to receive the Word.

"No man can come to me, except the father which hath sent me, draw him."
John 6:44

Pray that the Lord will till the soil of their heart until they are prepared to receive the Seed in *good ground*.

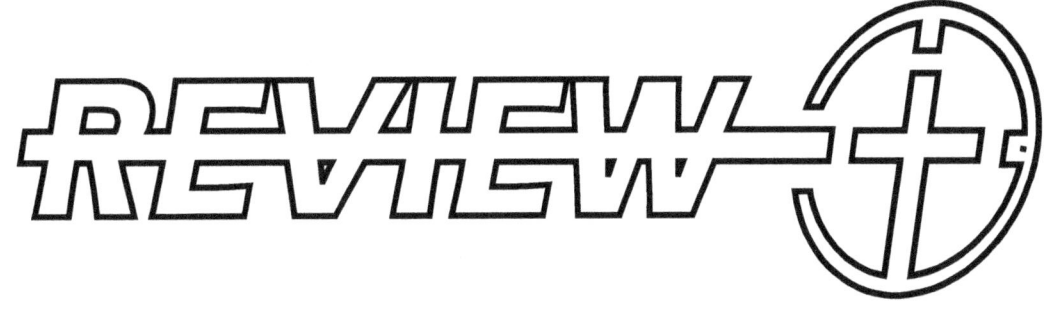

By Any Means

1. The Apostle Paul put his entire life's _____ at God's disposal for the sole purpose of reaching the lost.

2. Paul spoke the language of the _____ in order to direct the religious person to a saving knowledge of Jesus.

3. He was able to relate the Gospel of _____ to those who were in bondage.

4. He could converse in the language of the scholar to communicate the message of salvation to those who trusted in their _____.

5. Paul understood the importance of developing a _____ with the hearer by being able to relate through _____.

6. Your ability to _____ or _____ to an unbeliever will make you uniquely able to reach the heart of that person with the Gospel.

Relational Evangelism

1. Genuine evangelism springs from _____.

2. Practiced approaches and insincere presentations are easily read in inner city streets. Simply put; _____.

3. The effort to reach a soul is actually _____ with the Gospel.

4. Relational evangelism begins with the intent of _____ with the hearer; _____ and _____.

5. This type of evangelism transcends a prepared speech or _____ and moves into _____ that Jesus exemplifies in the Scriptures.

THE HARVEST PRINCIPLE

1. God has given a season for the initial planting or _____.

2. There is a time for watering, or _____ that Word which has already been planted.

3. And there is a time for harvesting; leading the seeker to a _____ of Jesus Christ.

4. The Planter, making _____.

5. The Waterer,_____ out the witness before the world.

6. The Harvester, leading the seeker in the _____ and ensuring that they are connected to the _____.

SECTION 4

HOOD-OLOGY

SHARING THE FAITH IN THE URBAN CONTEXT

Hood-ology *(a term coined by the late Evangelist Ron Haynes)* refers to an approach to ministry that meets the peculiar culture and needs of the inner-city...the *'hood*.

In this segment you will discover:
- How to determine the best method for sharing the gospel
- Your best personal approach for sharing the Faith
- Various techniques for presenting the gospel
- Biblical responses to common objections

CONTEXTUAL EVANGELISM

Evangelism in the urban context is as varied and complex as the people who share the inner city experience. The personality types are as diverse as they would be anywhere else, but the influences are different. There are circumstances that are peculiar to the urban experience that differentiate it from the suburbs. Themes of social justice, racial injustice, unemployment and crime have become part of the reality, and weigh heavily in the urban subconscious.

Sensitivity to the hopelessness and poverty, the influence of the drug and prison gang culture, and the predatory street culture that has resulted from them will help in knowing how to recognize and deal with the various personalities, and will also provide a credible platform for sharing the Faith.

There is no single *cookie-cutter* approach that applies in every situation. From the economically depressed and disenfranchised to the upwardly mobile and middle class home owners. From the Southern Bible Belt and Mid-western conservative to the West Coast liberal, the evangelistic approach will vary depending on traditions and cultural influences.

Evangelizing the urban context requires an understanding of the culture and the mind-set of those who live in marginalized communities. It also requires situational sensitivity or what we refer to as Cognitive Discernment.

COGNITIVE DISCERNMENT

Cognitive Discernment can be defined as engaging both your conscious awareness and your spiritual discernment in...

CONSCIOUS AWARENESS

This is the mental process of reading your surroundings. Through observing, you may be able to discern the needs of the prospect (the person with whom you are sharing the Faith) or a common concern that will help you to establish a connection.

It is important the prospect knows and feels you care about them or those things they are concerned about, and a perceptive glance may reveal those concerns.

Examples:

- Toys scattered around certainly indicate the presence of children. It may also indicate a need for child care.
- Alcohol bottles may indicate a casual drinker, or a person trying to drown their problems.
- Body posture may indicate a lack of receptivity, or they are busy and cannot spare the time or attention. This requires time in prayer, sensitivity to the Spirit of the Lord and sensitivity to the individual.

LEARN TO LISTEN - LISTEN TO LEARN

Everyone has issues they are coping with. Listen for the need in the individual and allow God's Spirit to lead you in tactful ways to approach them. Listen with a heart of compassion knowing that, while life is filled with questions, you have the answer... Jesus Christ.

SPIRITUAL DISCERNMENT

This requires that you are attuned to the Spirit of God through time spent in prayer and fasting prior to the actual outreach, preparing for the contingencies that may arise. You will be invading "enemy territory".

This also means that you must silence all the other voices in your mind that would distract you from hearing the voice of the Lord as you share the Faith.

With your spirit attuned to God's Spirit, you become spiritually aware of what God is doing in that moment.

BE OBSERVANT: listen, look and understand-

Flamboyant/boisterous personalities may indicate a need for recognition and respect, but may also indicate a fear of the lack of recognition and respect.

Dress may indicate gang affiliation or the desire to look the part.

The effective witness will learn the difference between a projected image and a genuine "Gangsta". Indicators will include gang colors, dress and tattoos which vary by region and type of gang.

Nervousness and avoidance of eye contact might suggest substance abuse, but be aware that in some cultures eye contact can be perceived as a challenge to authority and status.

Closed body posture and an aloof attitude may suggest an "I don't care" disposition, but may also indicate a fear of having their reality challenged.

The fast talking hustler personality may be more intelligent and knowledgeable than the image they project. They are *street wise* and may be watching for weaknesses to exploit.

Behind all of these personalities there is a person, a soul who needs to see the reality of the living Savior. Prayerfully look past the presentation to see that person (the abused-abandoned son or daughter, the person who has lost hope and faith, the person who only wants to be accepted) and try to reach the person behind the personality.

DISCERNING THE MOMENT

Evangelizing in the urban context requires a unique ability to read the moment; developing your observation skills and ability to discern your surroundings and the disposition of the person you are approaching.

Whether you have developed a relationship over a period of time, or you are making a "cold" approach, timing is essential. There is a time to engage a person, and there is a time to simply hand them a tract, say "God bless you" and walk away, depending on what is happening at that moment.

If the person appears to be under stress for any reason, their receptivity is not likely to be very good. Watch for signs of stress like tenseness, clenched teeth or nervousness. Be kind and show compassion by respecting their situation.

However, if they indicate a willingness to accept help by stopping and listening (even in the midst of the stressful situation) then by all means, share an encouraging word and offer to pray with them.

Always be aware of your surroundings. Simply stated—Learn to pray with your eyes open.

RECOGNIZING THE "GOD MOMENT"

In the course of sharing the faith, there comes a "God Moment" when the Lord is dealing with the heart of the seeker. This is a crucial time because they are at the point of accepting or rejecting the Savior, and you must be cognizant of this moment.

Examples of the "God Moment" could be:
- A change in body posture or facial expression
- Tears
- An earnest attempt to hear and understand what you are saying
- An expression of the frustration with their current situation, or they don't know what or whom to believe.

When your ability to perceive the moment intersects with their receptivity to the Spirit of God, this is the time to lead them to the Throne of Grace in prayer. If the seeker is not receptive at that moment, you might respectfully ask; "Would you mind if I pray for you?" If they agree, pray with them for the needs they have expressed or that you may have perceived, and then pray for them that the Lord will give them a desire to know Him as Savior and Lord.

SHARING THE FAITH

There are many methods or techniques that may be used in sharing the faith. From "THE FOUR SPIRITUAL LAWS" to "7 STEPS TO THE KINGDOM" the techniques for sharing the gospel message are as varied and adaptable as the individual presenting them. More important than the presentation of the gospel message is the message of the gospel in the presentation. In practicing techniques and applying methods, we must remember our main purpose is to share a message of hope...the message of salvation.
The essence of that message is found in this key verse of Scripture;

"For God so loved the world, that he gave his only begotten Son that whosoever believeth on him should not perish, but have everlasting life." (John 3:16)

In the urban context, God's love must be the motivating factor. Condescending glares, and insensitive comments do little to win a person who already feels disenfranchised by society or abandoned by the church. The "whosoever" must be inclusive of those persons — though they may not fit in our "Christianized" paradigm— who are willing to receive the free gift of God's Grace.

While we have included a sampling of techniques for sharing the Faith, as well as a brief overview of Scriptural responses to potential objections, be aware no recitation or repeating of Scripture brings about salvation. According to Romans 10:9-10, this only takes place when the person willingly embraces the truth of the gospel message and confesses Jesus as Savior and Lord.

So as you learn these techniques, remember they serve only to help you recall the Scriptures that are pertinent to soul winning. Be flexible enough to go "off-script" if the need arises, and minister Jesus to the individuals' immediate need. Let the sacrificial love that God has for this world be your motivator; let compassion and empathy shape your words; and let the love that God has placed in your heart enable you to reach the heart of the hearer.

THE ROMAN ROAD

ROMANS 3:23

"For all have sinned and come short of the Glory of God."

DIALOGUE:

(Restate the Scripture in your own words)

The Bible says that we have all sinned. Not one of us measures up to God's standard.

ROMANS 6:23

"For the wages of sin is death, but the gift of God is eternal life through Jesus Christ our Lord."

DIALOGUE:

(In your own words)

The bad news is that according to God's Word, the wages of sin is death. But the good news is that God has made provision for us; the gift of God is eternal life through Jesus Christ.

ROMANS 10:9

"That if thou shalt confess with thy mouth the Lord Jesus, and shalt believe in thine heart that God hath raised Him from the dead, thou shalt be saved."

DIALOGUE:

(Conclude in your own words)

If you can believe in your heart that Jesus died for your sins, and that God raised Him up from the dead; and if you are willing to confess Him as Saviour and Lord, you can have eternal life right now.

The Facts of Life

GOD LOVES YOU.

> The Bible says, in John 3:16; "For God so loved the world, that He gave his only begotten Son, that whosoever believeth on Him should not perish but have everlasting life."

MAN IS SINFUL BY NATURE, AND SEPARATED FROM GOD.

> The Bible says in Romans 3:23; "For all have sinned and come short of the Glory of God."

JESUS CHRIST IS THE ONLY ONE WHO CAN SAVE MAN.

> The Bible says in Acts 4:12; "Neither is their salvation in any other: for there is none other name under heaven given among men, whereby we must be saved."
>
> The Bible says in Romans 5:8; "God demonstrated his love toward us in that while we were yet sinners, Christ died for us."

YOU CAN BE SAVED BY FAITH IN THE LORD JESUS CHRIST.

> The Bible says in Romans 10:9; "That if thou shalt confess with thy mouth the Lord Jesus and shalt believe in thine heart that God raised Him from the dead, thou shalt be saved."

YOU CAN KNOW THAT YOU ARE SAVED.

> The Bible says in 1 John 5:11-12; "And this is the record that God hath given us eternal life and this life is in his Son. He that hath the Son hath life and he that hath not the Son hath not life."

As Easy As ABC

A — We must ACKNOWLEDGE our sins.

> The Bible says in 1 John 1:8-9; "If we say we have no sin, we deceive ourselves, and the truth is not in us." "If we confess our sins, He is faithful and just to forgive us our sins, and to cleanse us from all unrighteousness."
>
> The Bible says in Romans 3:23; "For all have sinned and come short of the glory of God."

B — We must BELIEVE that Jesus is Lord.

> The Bible says in Acts 16:31; "...believe on the Lord Jesus Christ, and thou shalt be saved."

C — We must CONFESS Jesus as our Lord.

> The Bible says in Romans 10:9; "That if thou shalt confess with thy mouth the Lord Jesus and shalt believe in thine heart that God raised Him from the dead, thou shalt be saved."

Common Objections
Biblical Responses

I NEED TO GET MY LIFE STRAIGHT BEFORE I CAN BE SAVED-

You need to be saved, in order to get your life straight. The Bible says in 2 Corinthians 5:17; "Therefore if any man be in Christ, he is a new creature: old things are passed away, behold all things are become new."

I'M TOO SINFUL-

By acknowledging your sins, you've already taken the first step toward being saved. The Bible says in 1 Tim.1:15; "Christ Jesus came into the world to save sinners." Would you like to pray with me to receive forgiveness now?

I'M NOT READY-

The Bible says in 2 Corinthians 6:2; "...behold, now is the accepted time; behold, now is the day of salvation." I appreciate the fact that you're not taking this lightly. May I leave this (tract/reading material) with you, so that when you decide, you'll know how to receive the Lord? Would you mind if we pray with you now?

IT'S TOO LATE, I'VE DONE TOO MUCH WRONG-

The Bible says in Hebrews 7:25; "...he is able also to save them to the uttermost that come unto God by him, seeing he ever liveth to make intercession for them." No matter how far you've gone, Jesus is standing at the right hand of God, pleading on your behalf. All you need to do is come to him to receive his forgiveness. Would you like to pray with me to receive forgiveness now?

A JUST AND LOVING GOD WOULDN'T CONDEMN A PERSON JUST BECAUSE THEY'RE NOT A CHRISTIAN-

The Bible says in John 3:17-18; "For God sent not his son into the world to condemn the world, but that the world through him might be saved." "He that believeth on him is not condemned: but he that believeth not is condemned already, because he hath not believed in the name of the only begotten son of God." It's true that God's intent is not to condemn the world, but he has made a provision for our salvation through his Son Jesus Christ. When we reject God's provision by not receiving that salvation, we actually condemn ourselves. Would you like to receive salvation now?

Tactical Tips

Model the Behavior
Behavior, appearance and deportment are your most effective tools for witnessing. Before people can see the Jesus in the Bible, they must see the Jesus in you.

Avoid Arguments About Religion
We are in a battle to win a soul...not an argument.
We are not promoting a religion, but salvation
Understand when a person just wants to debate or argue a point. Leave them a tract and calmly walk away.

Always Work in Teams
Always work with two or three team members.
One person should be the speaker, engaging the listener. The second stands with the Bible open to the referenced scripture, and the third is silently praying, listening for pertinent information, ready to record data on a 3x5 card.

Be Prepared
After a person has received Jesus as Savior, always assure them of God's forgiveness and salvation with Scripture.
Refer them to Romans 10:9 or 1 John 5:11-12.
Always bring pencils/pens and several 3x5 index cards to record important information (name, contact information, prayer requests, etc.)
Always provide reading material to leave with the listener: tracts, Bibles or booklets with your church's contact information; address, phone number, service times, etc.

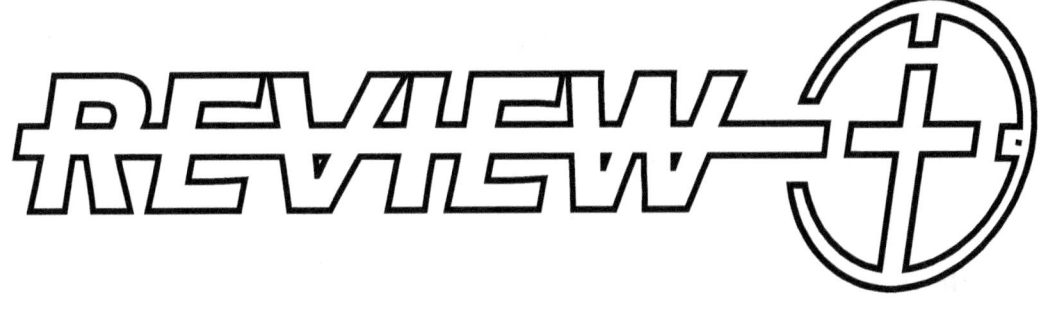

COGNITIVE DISCERNMENT

1. Cognitive Discernment can be defined as engaging both your _____ _____ and your _____. This is the mental process of _____ your surroundings. Through observing, you may be able to discern _____ of the prospect (the person with whom you are sharing the Faith) or a common concern that will help you to _____.

2. Everyone has issues they are coping with. Listen for the _____ in the individual and allow God's Spirit to lead you in tactful ways to approach them. Listen with a heart of _____.

3. You must be sensitive to the _____. This requires that you are attuned to the Spirit of God through time spent in _____ and _____ prior to the actual outreach, preparing for the contingencies that may arise.

4. This also means that you must silence all the other _____ that would distract you from hearing the voice of the Lord as you share with the individual.

5. With your spirit attuned to God's Spirit, you become _____ of what God is saying and doing in the life of the seeker- what He is doing in that _____.

6. Understanding urban culture and the mind-set of those who live in marginalized communities requires _____ and _____ sensitivity, or recognizing where you are and who you're talking to.

7. Understanding the impact of _____ and _____, the influence of the drug and prison _____ culture, and the predatory "_____" mentality that has resulted from them will help in knowing how to recognize and deal with the various personalities.

8. Flamboyant/boisterous personalities may indicate a need for _____ and _____, but may also indicate a fear of the *lack* of recognition and respect.

9. Dress may indicate _____ or the desire to *look* the part. The effective witness will learn the difference between a projected _____ and a genuine "Gangsta". Indicators will include _____, dress and _____ which vary by region and type of gang.
10. Nervousness and avoidance of eye contact might suggest _____ abuse, but be aware that in some cultures, eye contact can be perceived as a challenge to _____ and status.
11. Closed body posture and an aloof attitude may suggest an "I don't care" disposition, but may also indicate a fear of having their reality _____.
12. The fast talking _____ personality may be more _____ and knowledgeable than the image they project. They are _____ and may be watching for _____ to exploit.
13. Behind all of these personalities there is a _____ ; a soul who needs to see the reality of the living _____. Prayerfully look past the _____ to see that _____ and try to reach the *person* behind the personality.
14. Evangelizing in the urban context requires a unique ability to_____ _____; developing your observation skills and ability to _____ your _____ and the _____ of the person you are approaching.
15. Whether you have developed a relationship over a period of time, or you are making a "cold" approach, _____ is essential. There is a time to _____ a person, and there is a time to simply _____, say, "God bless you" and walk away, depending on what is happening at that moment.
16. If the person appears to be under stress for any reason, their _____ is not likely to be very good. Watch for signs of _____ like tenseness, clenched teeth or nervousness. Be _____ and show _____ by respecting their situation.

17. Always be aware of your surroundings. Put another way; "_____ _____."

18. In the course of sharing the faith, there comes a "_____" when the Lord is dealing with the heart of the prospect. This is a _____ time, because they are at the point of _____ or _____ the Savior, and you <u>must</u> be cognizant of this moment.

19. When your ability to _____ the moment intersects with their _____ to the Spirit of God, this is the time to lead them to the Throne of Grace in prayer.

20. If the seeker is not receptive at that moment, you might respectfully ask, "_____?" If they agree, pray *with* them for the needs they have expressed or that you may have perceived, and then pray *for* them that the Lord will give them a desire to know Him as Savior and Lord.

List four (4) examples of the "God Moment":

- _____.
- _____.
- _____.
- _____.

PRACTICE SHARING THE ROMAN ROAD

Romans____:_____

"For all have sinned and come short of the Glory of God."

Romans ___:____

"For the wages of sin is death, but the gift of God is eternal life through Jesus Christ our Lord."

Romans ____:___-_____

"...if thou shalt confess with thy mouth the Lord Jesus, and shalt believe in thine heart that God hath raised Him from the dead, thou shalt be saved."

God Loves You.

The Bible says, in John 3:16;

Man is sinful by nature, and separated from God.

The Bible says in Romans 3:23;

Jesus Christ is the only one who can save man.

The Bible says in Acts 4:12; The Bible says in Romans 5:8;

You can be saved by faith in the Lord Jesus Christ.

The Bible says in Romans 10:9;

You can know that you are saved.

The Bible says in 1 John 5:11-12;

A. We must _____ our sins.

The Bible says in 1 John 1:8-9;

The Bible says in Romans 3:23;

B. We must BELIEVE that _____.

The Bible says in Acts 16:31;

C. We must _____ Jesus as our _____.

The Bible says in Romans 10:9;

Common Objections
Biblical Responses

1. I need to get my life straight before I can be saved-
   The Bible says in 2 Corinthians 5:17;

2. I'm too sinful-
   The Bible says in 1Tim.1:15;

3. I'm not ready-
   The Bible says in 2 Corinthians 6:2;

4. It's too late, I've done too much wrong-
   The Bible says in Hebrews 7:25;

5. A just and loving God wouldn't condemn a person just because they're not a Christian-
   The Bible says in John 3:17-18;

TACTICAL TIPS

1. Model the Behavior _____, _____ and deportment are your most effective tools for witnessing. Before people can see the Jesus in the Bible, they must see _____.

2. Avoid Arguments About Religion- We are in a battle to_____ _____not an argument. We are not promoting a religion, but _____.

3. Understand when a person just wants to _____ or _____ a point. Leave them a tract and calmly _____.

4. Always Work in Teams-Always work with _____or _____ team members.

5. Only _____ person should be the initial speaker, engaging the listener. The second stands with the _____ open to the _____, and the third is silently _____, listening for _____, ready to record data on a 3x5 card.

6. Be Prepared- After a person has received _____(accepted the truth of the Word and prayed a repentance prayer), always assure them of _____ and _____ with _____.

7. Refer them to _____ or _____.

8. Always bring _____ and several _____ to record important information (name, contact information, prayer requests, etc.).

9. Always provide _____ to leave with the listener: tracts, Bibles or booklets with your churches contact information; address, phone number, service times, etc.

EVANGELISTIC STYLES PERSONALITY PROFILE
Discovering Your Best Ministry Method

On the following pages is an exercise designed to determine your best approach in personal evangelism. The statements in this exercise primarily deal with your self-perception (the way you see yourself), so there are no wrong answers. Please answer each question, and do not leave blank spaces as this will affect the final score and compromise the accuracy of your profile. Add the total of your scores across each row from left to right on the Evangelistic Styles Calculator and examine the results to see which style best suits you.

***Note:** This exercise is not intended as a psychological study of your personality, but is only meant to provide a general guideline for your best potential in personal evangelism.

EVANGELISTIC STYLES PERSONALITY PROFILE
Discovering your Best Ministry Method

Please record your response to these statements as you think they apply to you.
0- Does not apply 1- Barely applies 2-To some extent 3-Absolutely

1. I like to get right to the point ☐
2. I like to check out the facts behind a story ☐
3. I don't have a problem talking about my personal experiences ☐
4. I would rather talk about "real life issues" than to discuss a Bible study ☐
5. I would rather have someone with more experience explain Christianity to my friends ☐
6. I would rather get something done than to waste time talking about it ☐
7. I like staying informed on current issues ☐
8. I would talk about my own experiences in order to make a point ☐
9. I would rather talk to a person about what's happening in their life than to talk about what they believe ☐
10. I like to get people involved in what I'm doing ☐
11. People would say that I'm aggressive ☐
12. I like to think things through before I comment ☐
13. I would tell people about problems I've overcome, if I thought it would help them to overcome theirs ☐
14. I enjoy having meaningful discussions with friends ☐
15. I keep an eye out for events or interesting books that I think someone else might enjoy or profit from ☐
16. I would tell a person the truth, even if it meant losing their friendship ☐
17. I think it's important to have a good understanding of what you believe ☐
18. People would say that I relate well to others ☐
19. I seem to make friends easily ☐
20. I look for interesting Christian events to invite people to ☐
21. I don't have a problem putting a person on the spot ☐
22. People would say that I'm analytical ☐
23. People seem interested when I tell them how I came to the Lord ☐
24. People would say that I am a "people" person ☐
25. It would really "make my day" to have a friend come to church with me ☐
26. I believe in telling the truth, even if it hurts the person I'm telling ☐
27. I enjoy a good discussion on religious beliefs ☐
28. I'm still amazed at the way God saved me, and I love telling others about it ☐
29. I genuinely care about what happens to other people ☐
30. People would say I'm an engaging person ☐

EVANGELISTIC STYLES PERSONALITY PROFILE

Discovering your best Ministry Method

(Transfer the scores from the questionnaire to the corresponding numbers on the chart below, then add the numbers across each row to determine which evangelistic style most fits your personality)

EVANGELISTIC STYLES CALCULATOR

	Score		Score		Score		Score		Score		Score	Total	Style
1		6		11		16		21		26			Confrontational
2		7		12		17		22		27			Intellectual
3		8		13		18		23		28			Testimonial
4		9		14		19		24		29			Relational
5		10		15		20		25		30			Invitational

My best approach style is:

Adapting Your Style

Adapt your approach to the type of evangelism that best suits your personality.

Confrontational

- This technique serves best in door to door and street evangelism. *This person should remember compassion and empathy.*

Intellectual

- The intellectual technique serves best to the person who is well versed in Christian Apologetics (historical and philosophical arguments) used to support the Faith. *This person should remember that salvation is not an act of the intellect, but conversion is only accomplished by the Holy Spirit and takes place in the heart.*

Testimonial

- The testimonial technique is more suited to the person who is willing to open themselves to others in sharing the "before and after" of how their lives were changed after meeting Jesus. *This person should be careful not to reveal too much personal information, but keep the subject matter general and Christ-centered.*

Relational

- The relational technique is for the outgoing personality who knows how to make a friend and is willing to win a friend in order to win a soul. *This person should remember not to allow the development of the friendship to overshadow their purpose, which is to share the Gospel.*

Invitational

- One of the most commonly used techniques, invitational witnessing only requires asking an acquaintance to be your guest at a church event or worship service. *This person should follow up to ensure that their guest received or remains open to the Gospel.*

SECTION 5

The MINISTRY OF PRAYER

LEADING A SOUL TO SALVATION

The most critical instance in the evangelistic process is that moment which leads the prospective seeker to a saving relationship with Jesus Christ through the ministry of prayer.

In this segment you will learn:
- The power of prayer in the evangelistic process
- How to lead a person to salvation through prayer
- How you can assure a person of salvation through Scripture

The Ministry of Prayer

The Power of Prayer

In Soul Winning, we must maintain an attitude of prayerfulness.

We are invading *enemy territory*, and must be prepared both mentally and spiritually.

> "For we wrestle not against flesh and blood, but against principalities, against powers, against the rulers of the darkness of this world...." Ephesians 6:12

The Power of Compassion

Prayer has been called the sincere desire of the heart. We must sincerely desire salvation for the souls we are praying with.

We must have a genuine compassion for the souls of the people we are ministering to.

We must see them as God sees them; A soul in need of a Savior.

The Power of Faith

When we pray with a seeker, we are actually putting our faith to work for them, that God will give them eternal life.

> "But as many as received Him, to them gave He power to become the son's of God." John 1:12

We must have faith in our own ability to touch heaven for the unbeliever. We must believe that it is God's desire to give them eternal life.

> "Fear not, little flock; for it is your Father's good pleasure to give you the kingdom." Luke 12:32

The Ministry of Prayer (cont.)

The Nature of Prayer

There are many types of prayer for many occasions, but the nature of this prayer is unique in that it ushers a seeker into the presence of God, confirms the Scriptures, and directly relates to God's plan of Salvation as faith during this prayer actually transforms lives.

Leading a seeker to salvation through prayer

At the point in your witness that the person has indicated they are willing to give Jesus Christ lordship over their lives, they are ready to be lead in prayer (whether they know it or not). You ask; "Will you pray with me?"

Ask them to repeat the prayer with you. As you begin to pray, make sure you speak slowly and clearly, and then wait for them to repeat the prayer with you.

Note that each phrase of the prayer is directly related to the scriptures shared on pages 41-43 in the previous chapter.

As they repeat the prayer with you, in effect, they are agreeing with what the Bible says- and agreeing with you in prayer.

After you end the prayer, be sure to encourage them that (if they really meant what they said) God heard them, and they have eternal life- NOW- through Jesus Christ. (You may want to show them in the Scripture.)

1John 5:11-13
"And this is the record, that God hath given to us eternal life, and this life is in His Son." "He that hath the Son hath life; and he that hath not the Son of God hath not life." "These things have I written unto you that believe on the name of the Son of God; that ye may know that ye have eternal life..."

THE MINISTRY OF PRAYER (cont.)

FOLLOW UP

Equally as important as leading a seeker to the Savior, is the responsibility to make sure they gain a solid understanding of their new relationship with the Lord, and are securely connected in fellowship with other Believers in the Body of Christ.

It is essential they are contacted by you or a member of your church within a few days of their having received Christ. They may not wish to join your church, but encourage them to be your guest at church on the next available Sunday.

Be sure to get their name and address. Leave them with an encouraging tract, including church service times, contact numbers and directions to your church.

PRAY

Lord Jesus, I admit that I am a sinner and cannot save myself.

I believe that you are the Son of God and that you died for my sins.

I ask you to forgive me. Take control of my life and make me the kind of person you want me to be.

I receive You now, as my Lord and Savior.

Thank You for forgiving my sins and giving me eternal life.

Amen

SECTION

DEFENDING The FAITH

THE URBAN APOLOGETIC

There are some challenges to The Faith that are peculiar to the urban experience. While we don't advocate debates and arguments, we hold that there is a need to address crucial and critical questions.

In this lesson we
- All religions lead to God.
- The Bible was written by men.
- Jesus never existed.
- Christianity supports slavery.

DEFENDING THE FAITH

ALL RELIGIONS LEAD TO GOD -*Religious Pluralism*

Religious Plurality is based in the belief that God exists in many expressions. Whether as Heavenly Father; Universal Mind; Cosmic Consciousness; or the Divine Spark in humanity, they are all manifestations of the One God. Pluralism states that while all faiths believe they have exclusive truth, genuine faith can be nurtured without claiming exclusive truth. *

Webster's dictionary defines *truth* as the true or actual state of matter; conformity with fact or reality; or a verified undisputable fact.

By definition, truth is not all-inclusive but exclusive, distinguishing itself from everything that is not truth.

According to their own histories, almost every belief system was founded on an exclusive revelation of God, an exclusive understanding of what God requires, or an exclusive approach to how mankind is required to relate to God. The idea that all religions lead to God is in direct contrast to Jesus' claim to be the only (exclusive) way to God. *"Jesus saith unto him, I am the way, the truth, and the life: no man cometh unto the Father, but by me." John 14:6*

Almost every other belief system revolves around the human capacity to attain *enlightenment or oneness with* God through rituals, behavior modification, repetition of mantras, or through invoking ancestral spirits…but none of them offer salvation. Jesus' coming was to offer salvation through the sacrifice of Himself; *"For He hath made Him to be sin for us, who knew no sin; that we might be made the righteousness of God in Him." 2 Cor. 5:21.*

It is not the Christian, but it is the Christ who claims to be the only way to God. So the argument that faith can be nurtured without claiming exclusivity is rendered invalid, because it is impossible to express faith in the Christ of the Bible without claiming exclusivity.

---

*Friedman, Thomas. The Real War, New York Times, Nov. 27, 2001

Defending The Faith (cont.)

THE BIBLE WAS WRITTEN BY MEN – The authenticity of the Scriptures

Every book that has been written, was written by men. The question becomes; "Is the Bible the Word of God?"

While many books are called "holy" or said to contain the words of God, the Bible is the only one recorded by over forty (40) different writers who lived at different times throughout history; who lived in different places; who came from diverse backgrounds; who didn't confer with one another, but wrote one continuous narrative. From Genesis to Revelations, the Bible is the record of God's plan to reconcile mankind to Himself through Jesus Christ. The authenticity of the Bible is shown in its own history and the fact that its revelation was not restricted to any one individual or secret order.

"Knowing this first, that no prophecy of the Scripture is of any private interpretation. For the prophecy came not in old time by the will of man: but holy men of God spake as they were moved by the Holy Ghost" 2 Peter 1:20-21.

The original Scriptures were meticulously copied in exacting detail which included specific instructions for the size and number of the columns, the spacing between the words, the lines of print and the number of letters. The scribes who were charged with this responsibility were prohibited from writing anything from memory. The spaces, lines and letters were numbered and counted methodically, and if one mistake was found the entire manuscript was discarded as faulty and destroyed.*

It wasn't the chapters or the verses that were copied, but every letter and every space. According to Deuteronomy 31:24-28, Moses commissioned the Levites to maintain the Scriptures in a compartment of the Ark of the Covenant, sealing them from being "tampered" with.

---

*The Apologetics Study Bible. Holman Bible publishing, Nashville, Tenn. 2007

In 1947, a series of biblical scrolls were discovered in a cave near the Dead Sea. These "Dead Sea Scrolls" were determined to be at least one thousand years older than the earliest copies of the Hebrew Scriptures. After a comparative study, it was concluded that the scrolls were 95% word for word accurate, with the remaining 5% error being differences in spelling. The meaning and context of the texts in the Scriptures and the discovered manuscripts were identical, supporting the accuracy of the biblical copies with no changes or differences in context.[†]

[†] McDowell, Josh; the New Evidence That Demands A Verdict, Thomas Nelson Publishing 1999

DEFENDING THE FAITH (cont.)

JESUS NEVER EXISTED - The reality of Jesus

The proof that Jesus existed can be found in the record of secular (or non-Christian) historians of the first and second century A.D.

Among those who wrote about Jesus were historians Flavius Josephus and Cornelius Tacitus; and Greek satirist Lucian.

In the book *Antiquities,* Josephus writes;

"Now, about this time Jesus, a wise man, if it be lawful to call him a man, for he was a doer of wonderful works- a teacher of such men as receive the truth with pleasure. He drew over to him both many of the Jews and many of the Gentiles." *

In 116 A.D. Cornelius Tactitus wrote concerning the burning of Rome, which had been attributed to the Emperor Nero;

"Therefore, to scotch this rumour, Nero substituted as culprits, and punished with the utmost refinements of cruelty, a class of men, loathed for their vices, whom the crowd styled Christians. Christus, the founder of the name, had undergone the death penalty in the reign of Tiberius, by sentence of the procurator Pontius Pilatus."

In 170 A.D. Lucian the Satirist wrote;

"The Christians, you know, worship a man to this day- the distinguished personage who introduced their novel rites, and was crucufied in that account ... you see, these misguided creatures start with the general conviction that they are immortal for all time, which explains the contempt of death and voluntary self-devotion which are so common among them; and then it was impressed on them by their original lawgiver that they are all brothers, from the moment they are converted, and deny the gods of Greece, and worship the crucified sage, and live after his laws."†

---

*Josephus the Complete Works, translated by William Whiston, A.M. Thomas Nelson publishers, Nashville, 1998

† McDowell, Josh, Wilson, Bill; Evidence for the Historical Jesus. Harvest House Publishers, Oregon. 1993

In these works, Josephus verifies the historical existence of Jesus, Tacitus supports the fact that Jesus was crucified by Pontius Pilate, and (without intending to) Lucian substantiates the biblical record that Jesus was worshipped as the Son of God. Among the archeological discoveries that substantiate the biblical account of Jesus' life are the discovery in 1961 of an inscription from Pontius Pilate "Prefect of Judea" and the excavation of the small town of Nazareth in 1962. Both of these support the historicity of the biblical events in proving that the people and the places spoken of in the Bible actually existed.

The Hebrew Scriptures speak of the coming of the Messiah who would reconcile man to God. In Isaiah 7:14, the prophet recorded this word, "Therefore the Lord Himself will give you a sign: Behold the virgin shall conceive and bear a Son, and shall call His name Immanuel."

Micah writes, "But thou, Bethlehem Ephratah, thougfh thou be little among the thousands of Judah, yet out of thee shall he come forth unto me that is to be ruler in Israel; whose goings forth have been from old, from everlasting." (Micah 5:2)

In Zechariah 9:9, the prophet foretells the arrival of the Messiah on a colt, " Rejoice greatly, O daughter of Zion; shout, O daughter of Jerusalem: behold thy King cometh unto thee: he is just, and having salvation; lowly, and riding upon an ass, and upon a colt the foal of an ass."

And, again, Isaiah the prophet gives detail to the betrayal, rejection, scourging and death that would be endured by the Messiah. (Isaiah 53)

According to the gospel, and the historic narratives of secular writers; these prophecies were fulfilled, to the letter, in Jesus of Nazareth.

The Old Testament Scriptures had been sealed in the Temple at Jerusalem for at least 400 years, prior to the life of Jesus (450-400 B.C.) So, the prophetic writings concerning the Messiah could not have been altered, at least not without a conspiracy that would include the cooperation of the Jewish Priests and Scribes; a complete compromise and controverting of the Talmud which secured the purity and accuracy of the Hebrew texts, and an investigator who could track and catalogue every event in the life of Jesus and then insert those events in the prophetic texts in the style and language of each prophet.

Just as it is with the authenticity of the Scriptures; the life and the ministry, as well as the crucifixion and the worship of Jesus are all validated by history, archeology and by the prophetic record.

Defending The Faith (cont.)

Christianity and Slavery - Does Christianity support slavery?

As reprehensible as the idea is to modern thinking, slavery has existed since before recorded history and was a functional part of practically every civilization (including that of Arabic Muslims). Instructions for the treatment of slaves (called bondmen or bondwomen) were included in the ancient Assyrian and Sumerian texts, the Code of Hammurabi and the Laws of Moses.

There was, however, a marked difference between the slavery of ancient times, and what we have come to know as slavery today. In ancient times, there were four primary methods by which a person might become a slave. One might be a captive of war, set to work for the conquering nation.(Deut 20:14; 21:10-14; 2 Ki 5:2; 2 Chron 28:8-10). One might be sentenced to servitude for a crime (mostly theft). (Gen 43:18; Ex 22:3). A person could willfully sell themselves or their children to make restitution for a debt (Le 25:39; Mt 18:25), or one could sell themselves into slavery to a wealthy owner to escape poverty.

The Hebrew Scriptures neither condoned nor condemned the practice, but (much like murder or divorce) the laws only addressed conduct under the circumstance.

The Bible makes a difference, however, between these methods of acquiring bondservants and what the Scriptures refer to as "man-stealing" (the willful act of kidnapping a person for the sole purpose of selling them into slavery- much like the 19th century slave traders who kidnapped Africans to sell in the "New World"). In fact, the Bible speaks out so strongly in this instance, that the perpetrators of such crimes were sentenced to death. "And he that stealeth a man, and selleth him, or if he be found in his hand, he shall surely be put to death." Ex 21:16

Slavery was opposed by the early Christian church as contradictory to the teachings of the Bible. First century historian, Clement notes that Christians in opposition to slavery allowed themselves to be sold into servitude to secure liberty for others; "We know many among ourselves who have given themselves up to slavery, in order that they could ransom others."

In the Apostolic Constitutions of 390, Christians were instructed to avoid places where slaves were sold, unless they intended to purchase them to set them at liberty.

"A believer should not go to any of those public meetings, unless to purchase a slave and to save a soul… such sums of money as are collected from them [should] be used for the redemption of the saints and the deliverance of slaves and captives." [*]

The idea that Christianity was created to enslave Africans stands in direct contrast with the fact that some American slaveholders resisted the "Christianizing" of their slaves for fear that a Christian slave might be set free by law. To reinforce this order, Black preachers - both slave and free - were outlawed in most southern states.[†]

In Luke 4:18, Jesus makes His position on slavery clear. "The Spirit of the Lord is upon me, because He hath anointed me to preach the Gospel to the poor; He hath sent me to heal the brokenhearted, to preach deliverance to the captives, and recovering of sight to the blind, to set at liberty them that are bruised." This was/is God's message; deliverance to the captive, and liberty for them that are bruised. One can only equate the gospel with freedom.

---

[*]Bercot, David W. A Dictionary of Early Christian Beliefs. Hendrickson Publishers, 1998
[†]Harley, Sharon. The Timetables of African-American History. Simon & Schuster, 1996

DEFENDING THE FAITH (cont.)

AFRICANS CAME TO CHRISTIANITY THROUGH SLAVERY - How did Christianity come to Africans?

The concept that Africans (and African Americans in particular) were introduced to Christianity through the institution of slavery is a major misconception.

Christianity had spread throughout North Africa, establishing churches in Libya, Egypt, and Ethiopia, as early as the first century A.D. From the second to the sixth century, Christian Churches had been founded in Nubia, Axum and Swahili.

In tracing the growth of Western Civilization, historians only followed the missionary journeys of St. Paul to Greece, Rome and Italy. In the process, they totally ignored the work of St. Mark who established the first Christian churches in Alexandria, Egypt in 60 A.D. *

Only a few historians note the record of the eunuch who carried the Gospel to Ethiopia, as documented in the book of Acts 8:27. This story was confirmed by first century historian Eusebius. **

In his book, "The Wonders of the African World", Henry Louis Gates wrote "Ethiopia is not only the oldest continuous seat of Christianity after the Egyptian church on the Continent, but the second most frequently mentioned (after Egypt) African country in both the Old and New Testaments." †

According to the Bible, it was not European Christians who first brought the gospel to Africans, but African believers who first declared the gospel to the Greeks;

"Now they which were scattered abroad upon the persecution that arose about Stephen traveled as far as Phenice, and Cyprus, and Antioch preaching the Word to none but unto the Jews only. And some of them were men of Cyprus and Cyrene, which, when they were come to Antioch, spake unto the Grecians, preaching the Lord Jesus." Acts 11: 19,20

---

*Shillington, Kevin. History of Africa. St. Martin's Press, 1995
**Eusebius, Penguin books 1965
† Gates, Henry Louis, jr. Wonders of the African World. Alfred A. Knopf 1999.

Notes

NOTES

JDMorgan

JDMorgan is the founder and Executive Director of Urban Assault Outreach Ministry, an evangelistic ministry dedicated to developing and facilitating outreach and discipleship training in the urban context.

His ministry experience includes outdoor crusades throughout Northern California, prison outreach at San Quentin State Prison, Santa Rita Jail and the California Youth Correctional Facilities, as well as presentations as guest lecturer at American Baptist Seminary of the West-Berkeley, CA; Patten Bible College – Oakland CA , and Bethany Bible College- Santa Cruz CA.

An accomplished writer, JD is the author of Urban Assault: The WORD on the Street, Urban Assault: The Workbook, and To Follow Jesus (a twelve step study in Christian Discipleship). He also serves as a contributing writer for The Minister's Voice magazine of Fresno, California.

www.ingramcontent.com/pod-product-compliance
Lightning Source LLC
Chambersburg PA
CBHW080446110426
42743CB00016B/3300